The Orange
on the
P L A T E

A Liberated Seder

A woman-centered, open and affirming, interfaith,
multifaith, no faith, secular humanist seder.

BY LOIS HECKMAN
ILLUSTRATIONS BY ELLEN DESCHATRES

To order additional copies of this book, contact:
Xlibris
844-714-8691
www.Xlibris.com
Orders@Xlibris.com

ISBN: Softcover 978-1-4771-0362-3
EBook   978-1-4771-0363-0

Print information available on the last page

Rev. date: 12/15/2020

THOUGHTS AND THANKS

I have always been drawn to the story of Passover. I believe its because it relates to my progressive, political, feminist values, and is at its heart, the story of the struggle to freedom. I hoped to create a Seder that would be accessible to people of different faiths, and especially to atheists and agnostics. I did not want it to be a worship service, and I didn't want it to be too long!

I thank my friend and celebrant colleague Dorry Bless for her contributions to this text, and all her help and support.

Big thanks goes to my husband Kent, who puts up with, and even encourages me in all I do; and for cooking more than one large Passover dinner because of all this!

And finally, thanks goes to Ellen Deschatres, for coming into this project at the perfect moment and contributing her time and talent to bring this book to life with her charming illustrations.

INSTRUCTIONS AND IDEAS FOR CONDUCTING THIS SEDER

I suggest that the leader, after having familiarized herself with the text, give a brief over view of how the dinner will be co-mingled with the reading. Note that everyone will go around the table, taking turns reading from the text. Read as much or as little as you want, and, if you don't wish to read, that's ok, too. There should be no pressure whatsoever.

This Seder is designed to stop at various times to serve the different courses. As many may know, it can be difficult waiting to eat until finishing the reading of the Haggadah. It's fun to break up the sections with different courses of the meal! Feel free to improvise on this in whatever way you wish.

You will need the items for the Seder plate, which are a little different than the traditional items (refer to that section in our book) and one large wine glass, or Miriam cup, for sharing. Any plate will do, and you don't need a special cup either. It's up to you!

You can have men attend or keep it women only. It's a women's Seder either way because it tells the story from the perspective of the women of Exodus and focuses on women's issues. I look this way: perhaps it is men who need to hear this the most, to understand the struggles of women. But another way to look at it is that a women only event creates a safe space for women to share, outside the company of men. Again – it's up to you!

Another custom I've developed is to have a candle at each place setting and let everyone light their candle at the designated spot in the ceremony.

I hope you can add, embellish and adapt the Seder in any way that suits you, but most of all, I hope in this Seder you have found something special and new to love about Passover. If you've never conducted a Seder there are plenty of resources on-line to explain the foods and classic rituals. This might help put it in context, but remember, with *The Orange on the Plate* – freedom is the thing!

WELCOME

Welcome to our open and affirming, interfaith, multifaith, no faith, secular humanist women's Seder.

A traditional Seder is an ancient Jewish ritual feast marking the beginning of Passover. During the Seder the Passover story is told, and it is a story with universal implications – a story of oppression, struggle and freedom. Special food is eaten and Seders are enacted in various ways all over the world. A book, called a Haggadah, is used, and the family or group follows the book, taking turns reading, following the story of Passover along with prayers and other rituals. Seder means 'order' because the story is told in the same way generation after generation, so that the importance of the struggle for freedom will not be lost. We hope our Seder will also help perpetuate this great story.

The Seder is perhaps the most important Jewish ceremony conducted at home, which is probably why it is so well loved. There is wine, a special Seder plate with symbolic food items, and all kinds of different traditions abound. However, too often the Seder is long in duration, everyone is very hungry by the time they get to eat, and are reticent to resume the ceremonial portion by the evening's end. So we have intentionally crafted tonight's ritual granting ourselves freedom - one of the central messages of Passover - in the way we have re-interpreted the Passover tradition.

As we reinvent the Seder we invite ritual into our lives. Ritual allows us to mark the seasons of the year and the seasons of our lives. The act of ritual is a way for us to tell and retell the narrative in which our lives unfold. Ritual is one of the ways we emotionally transmit stories and values.

It connects us to our ancestors, to each other, and in so doing transcends time. It helps us make sense of our world and of ourselves; and encourages us to express ourselves soulfully. And so now we come together in our own way: to share Passover, to enjoy food, wine, empowerment and each other.

To begin, let's go around the table and introduce ourselves, but in the following way… say ''my name is… daughter (or son) of….., who is the daughter of….' Go back as far as you are able, honoring the female lineage of your family, ancestry too often forgotten.

THE SEDER PLATE

The traditional Seder plate contains specific items. As we take turns reading, taste the foods as they are described. There is also a non-traditional item on the plate, and we'll explain that as well.

1. The first item is called Charoset (ha-ROE-set). It is mixture of apples, nuts, wine and spices. Charoset is symbolic of the mortar the Jewish slaves made in their building for the Egyptians.

2. There is usually **Zeroa** (zay-ROE-ah), a shank bone – but we're using a beet. It is symbolic of the lamb offered as the Passover sacrifice. We'll hear about that soon. We are using a beet, because when cut open it appears to bleed. For us it also symbolizes the blood of women.

3. The hard-boiled egg is called **Baitzah** (BAIT-za). It is symbolic of the sacrifices brought to the Temple in ancient times. Some have interpreted this as a symbol of mourning for the loss of the two great Jewish Temples (the first was destroyed by the Babylonians in 586 B.C.E., the second by the Romans in 70 C.E.). The egg symbolizes this loss and traditionally became the food of mourners. However another and perhaps more obvious symbolism of the egg is that of fertility and it is, therefore, a strong symbol of womanhood and life.

4. **Karpas** (Kar-pus) is any vegetable. Parsley is generally used and there is also a **bowl of salt water.** The Karpas is dipped in salt water to represent tears. The custom of serving karpas dates back to Jerusalem of the 1st and 2nd centuries when it was common to begin a formal meal by passing around vegetables as hors d'oeuvres. We will soon hear a story of many tears.

5. **Maror** (Mah-roar) is the name of the bitter herbs. Horseradish is generally used. Maror represents the bitter life of the Israelites during the time of their enslavement in Egypt. These are the traditional items.

6. **The Orange** In the early 1980s, while speaking at Oberlin College, a well-known Jewish feminist scholar, Susannah Heschel, was introduced to an early feminist Haggadah that suggested adding a crust of bread on the Seder plate, as a sign of solidarity with Jewish lesbians. Understand that there is *never* bread at Passover, but matzo, so the crust of bread was intended to convey the idea that there's as much room for a lesbian in Judaism as there is for a crust of bread on the Seder plate.

Heschel, however, felt that to put bread on the Seder plate would also be to say that Jewish lesbians and gay men *violate* Judaism like *hametz* (leavened food) violates Passover. Not a good symbol! So she came up with something better. At her next Seder, she chose an orange as a symbol of inclusion of gays and lesbians and others who are marginalized within the Jewish community. She offered the orange as a symbol of the fruitfulness for all Jews when lesbians and gay men are contributing and active members of Jewish life.

In addition, each orange segment had a few seeds that had to be spit out, as a gesture of spitting out, repudiating, the homophobia of Judaism. While lecturing, Heschel often mentioned her custom as one of many feminist rituals that have been developed in the last 20 years. Then something interesting happened. In a typical patriarchal maneuver, her idea of an orange and its intention of affirming lesbians and gay men got manipulated. A story circulated that a man said to Heschel that 'a woman belongs on the bimah (the podium of a synagogue) as much as an orange belongs on the Seder plate.' So a woman's words became attributed to a man, and the affirmation of lesbians and gay men was erased. Isn't that precisely what's happened over the centuries to women's ideas? But not tonight! Let's us now light the candles, and let them bring new light to the world.

FIRST RITUAL CUP OF WINE – MIRIAM'S CUP

We also have a special cup on our Passover table – called Miriam's cup. Let the wine bring new joy into our hearts.

(Pour a huge glass of wine while the following is read, taking turns and passing around the cup for everyone to drink from)

The legend of Miriam tells of a mysterious well filled with 'living waters' and how it followed the Israelites as they wandered through the desert. We'll learn more about Miriam later in our Seder.

Miriam's Well was said to hold Divine power to heal and renew. Its fresh waters sustained the people as they were transformed from a generation shaped by slavery into a free nation. Think about the symbolic and poetic idea behind this story: a well, found and tended by a woman, which sustains her people.

Throughout their subsequent journeys… the many trials of the Jewish people… they will strive to rediscover these living waters. Soon we'll hear the story of Moses, placed in the water of the Nile, and the women who saved him. Water is a symbol of cleansing and new life. All cultures, religions and traditions have rituals using water. Our bodies are made up mostly of water, as is the earth. Water often symbolizes the unconscious and the feminine.

Perhaps, part of what the allegory of the Passover story offers is a way to revisit how we relate to the collective unconscious, and the feminine, and reflect on the ways they connect us all. When we look at the similarities of our life experience regardless of gender, religion, ethnicity, age, however we choose to define ourselves ---- we begin to see there are ways we can come together and live with a sense of hope and trust.

Buddha said: Let yourself be open and life will be easier. A spoon of salt in a glass of water makes the water undrinkable. A spoon of salt in a lake is almost unnoticed.

Taoism teaches: Nothing is softer or more flexible than water, yet nothing can resist it.

In the words of Leonardo DaVinci: "In rivers, the water that you touch is the last of what has passed and the first of that which comes; so with present time."

And writer, Alan Watts, said "To have faith is to trust yourself to the water. When you swim you don't grab hold of the water, because if you do you will sink and drown. Instead you relax, and float."

So let's remember to drink some water tonight, as well as our wine!

THE FOUR QUESTIONS

One of the most recognizable and memorable parts of a traditional Seder is the asking of the four questions. The youngest at the Seder table always does this. The overall question is: Why is this night different from all other nights? Here is the traditional way it usually goes…

1. Why is it that on all other nights we eat either bread or matzo, but on this night we eat only matzo? And the answer is: We eat only matzo because our ancestors could not wait for their breads to rise when they were fleeing slavery in Egypt, and so they took the breads out of their ovens while they were still flat, which was matzo.

2. Why is it that on all other nights we eat all kinds of herbs, but on this night we eat only bitter herbs? The answer given is: We eat only Moror, a bitter herb, to remind us of the bitterness of slavery that our ancestors endured while in Egypt.

3. Why is it that on all other nights we do not dip our herbs even once, but on this night we dip them twice? Answer: The first dip, green vegetables in salt water, symbolizes the replacing of tears with gratefulness, and the second dip, Moror in Charoses, symbolizes sweetening the burden of bitterness and suffering to lessen its pain.

4. Why is it that on all other nights we eat either sitting or reclining, but on this night we eat in a reclining position? Answer: We recline at the Seder table because in ancient times, a person who

reclined at a meal symbolized a free person, free from slavery, and so we recline in our chairs at the Passover Seder table to remind ourselves of the glory of freedom.

It is interesting to note that while the questions are asked and answered, more questions are always encouraged, as questioning in the Jewish tradition, is the way to learn. For example: "Rabbi, why do Jews answer a question with another question?" And the Rabbi replies, "Why not?"

Tonight, we ask not only why is this night different, but also how is it different for us?

1. When so many in our culture are pre-occupied with food to the point of obsession and still others are hungry, why do we celebrate with matzo tonight? Answer: On this night as we remember the Jewish women escaping slavery who took only unleavened bread – all they had time to take – and we gather to support all women still enslaved.

2. Why on this night, when so many in our culture are attached to seeking the 'perfect' life, do we speak of sadness? And the answer is: On this night we gather together, to share tears of joy and tears of sadness, in a way our foremothers could never have imagined.

3. When so many in our own culture and throughout the world are suffering, why do we express gratitude? Answer: On this night we free ourselves from the bitterness of the legacy of oppression and sweeten our lives with hope.

4. During this celebration of freedom -- why do we stop to ask when will we all really be free? The answer is: On this night we gather to support women, men, gay, lesbian and transgender people to be free to be themselves in our evolving world.

SECOND RITUAL CUP OF WINE

This cup of wine is dedicated to cleansing. Many of our mothers, and their mothers and their mothers' mothers, devoted themselves for days and weeks preparing for the Passover holiday. (The same can surely be said for women preparing for Easter or other holidays.) They cooked and cleaned making certain that every last crumb of 'hametz' was nowhere to be found. Perhaps our maternal ancestors felt enslaved to cleaning their homes, and to managing their households. Maybe some of us still feel this way.

For us tonight, around this table, if we look inside, we might realize we feel enslaved by others, their expectations of us, society; or possibly, by what we demand of ourselves. Sometimes, when we sit with our suffering, we see that it is our very own thoughts - all of the big and little ways in which we have been conditioned - that cause us pain.

So if we consider the Passover story again, we see how universal the feelings and experiences of enslavement, struggle and freedom are to being human. It happens around the world, both literally and figuratively.

And so now, if you feel inclined, please share a thought about yourself, your life and how you feel confined and/or where you feel free. As we share our experiences aloud, we are mindful that our foremothers were not encouraged to communicate in this way and that many women and girls all over the world do not have this freedom.

THE STORY OF THE EXODUS

How does the journey to freedom begin? The story of Passover took place 3,000 years ago in Egypt when the Pharaoh, an all-powerful king, enslaved the Israelites. Before we get to the lesser known story of the women, let's review the classic story; and its' four parts: the enslavement of the Israelites, the story of Moses, the Ten Plagues, and Exodus.

The Enslavement of the Israelites

The Hebrews (aka: the Israelites, the Jews) had gone to Egypt because there was a famine in Canaan and they had no food. But instead of returning home to Canaan, they stayed in Egypt for a long time - a familiar story still today. So, the number of Hebrews living in Egypt grew very large.

The Pharaoh, Ramses II, was worried about the growing influence of these Hebrews, just as some feel threatened by the changing color of America, and so he launched a plan of genocide – to kill Hebrew baby boys. He also enslaved the Hebrews, obviously a horrible turn of events, a horrific tale that sadly repeats itself for Jews and other groups throughout history. But today we are telling this story, which still is so relevant, and we'll continue the narrative most people are familiar with.

The Story of Moses

There was an Israelite couple who were expecting a baby and when they had a baby boy (whose name would later be Moses) they decided to hide him because they couldn't let anyone kill their beautiful, precious baby. So they hid Moses for three months, but as he got older it became harder to hide him, and they did the only thing they could think of, they made a basket and placed the basket in some tall grass in the Nile River and let him go, hoping for the best.

Moses' sister Miriam watched from a distance and she saw somebody coming. It was the Pharaoh's daughter with her servants. And in a history changing moment, Pharaoh's daughter saved Moses.

So Moses grew up in the lap of luxury, but he developed empathy for the slaves, and one day when he witnessed a slave being beaten by an Egyptian, and he couldn't stand it – he killed the Egyptian slave-master, and of course, he had to flee for his very life. He went to Midian, married and became a shepherd. He had a modest but good life, but God called on him – in an epic way - to become the leader of the Hebrews. His job: to free the Hebrew slaves! So he followed God's instructions and went back to Egypt to convince Pharaoh to free his people.

The Ten Plagues

But Pharaoh ignores his pleas. Moses warned him of the God's wrath, but Pharaoh didn't believe it. So God, the story goes, unleashed a series of 10 terrible plagues on the people of Egypt, and one by one, after each punishment, Moses repeated his plea to the Pharaoh. Let my people go!

The plagues were:

1. The water of River Nile turned into blood
2. Frogs
3. Lice or gnats
4. Wild Beasts (or maybe flies)
5. Disease on livestock
6. Boils
7. Hail mixed with fire
8. Locusts
9. Darkness
10. Death: the Slaying of the First Born

The first nine plagues only served to make the Pharaoh angry, and he did not free the slaves. So God sent the 10th and most horrible (and ironic) plague, but before ordering it, He instructed the Hebrew slaves to make a sacrifice of the lamb in the Holy Temple of Jerusalem and mark their doors with the blood of the lamb, as an indication to God to 'pass over' their houses while He would be busy slaying the first born males of the Egyptians.

The Hebrews did as instructed, and their first-born males were saved from the tenth plague. This is where the name Passover comes from; 'Pesach' means 'passing over' or 'protection' in Hebrew. This finally does it, and Pharaoh ordered the Israelites to be set free immediately and allows their passage to freedom, but soon after changed his mind, and sent his army chasing after them. The whole Red Sea incident happens here, Moses parts the sea, the Israelites cross, and the seas crash down upon the pursuing army, drowning them, and the Hebrews get away - you may have seen it in the movies!

The Exodus

In their hurry to flee (and who could blame them?) the Israelites didn't have time for their dough to rise so they could bake bread to take on their journey, and instead had to take raw dough. This dough got baked in hot desert sun, becoming hard crackers, which is our Matzo!

Ok, so we have a final triumph, and that is the basic story as most of us know it, not including the next part, where they wandered in the desert for 40 years, but that's another story entirely!

26

THE THIRD CUP OF WINE

Dedicate this cup of wine to a woman who inspires you.

We will go around the table and each of you can share a story of a 'woman of valor' - someone you know personally or a woman you admire currently or historically.

THE FIVE WOMEN OF EXODUS

So what were the women doing during the story of Exodus? Well there are five great women in the story you don't hear much about. They are: two Hebrew midwives, Moses' mother Jocheved (yo-HEV-ed), Moses' older sister, Miriam, and a princess of Egypt, Pharaoh's daughter.

Five women, by virtue of their gender have been marginalized, deemed not important to the history of a people. This great epic story of exodus is usually told from the perspective of Moses, the innocent little baby who floated down the Nile and grew up to lead his people to freedom.

But before Moses was ever born and emerged from that basket of bull rushes, there were five women who chose to misbehave in quiet yet subversive ways that made all of it possible. They were not great historic figures with prominent positions and lots of power. They were simply women who saw injustice and oppression and said no, in whatever way they could.

First there were Shiphrah (SHIF-rah) and Puah (POO-ah), who were midwives. They are usually not included on any top ten lists of biblical characters; even most people who know the bible are not familiar with them. We don't even know whether they were Hebrews or Egyptians, but we do know that their job was to tend to the Hebrew women whenever they went into labor.

In every society and every age there are women who take this role... accompanying a woman through the intense labor of delivering a baby, work that was for most of human history a remote mystery to men.

These are women who specialize in reproductive issues - they advised on pregnancy problems, mopped sweaty brows, delivered babies and cut cords and stopped bleeding.

Pharaoh thought that through the midwives he could stop the proliferation of the Hebrews, so he ordered two midwives, Shiphrah and Puah to kill any male babies born to Hebrew women. When the baby is delivered, he told them, get rid of it if it's a boy. It was a simple plan of genocide that, in Pharaoh's mind, would not be difficult to enact. And so he gave the order to the midwives, and then went back to dreaming big plans for building Egypt.

The third woman of Exodus is not even named in the book, but her name can be found in later passage... it was Jocheved. She was a Hebrew woman who was mother to at least one daughter and one son - Miriam and Aaron. It was in this climate of genocide that she found herself pregnant. We can only imagine how difficult it was to be pregnant in Egypt at that time. She probably had little choice about her pregnancy, and when she delivered a baby boy, she knew exactly what that meant: death.

The fourth woman of Exodus wasn't a woman at all, she was just a little girl. And her childhood was lived in the danger and violence of the Pharaoh's policies, the slavery of her people, and the heartbreaking grief of her mother. She wasn't that old, but she was old enough to know what was happening in her family, and old enough to become involved in her mother's desperate attempts to save her baby brother.

And finally, the fifth woman was a woman of the most elite class in the land. She was the daughter of the Pharaoh. She had every luxury at her disposal, endless servants to meet her every need. She was not occupied with thoughts of slavery or genocide or oppression or racism.

They were all different, these five women of Exodus. And they were all the same, because they each, in their own quiet way, put up a hand in the face of all the violence and death and injustice going on around them... and said no.

Shiphrah and Puah concocted the most ridiculous story for the Pharaoh... "You know those Hebrew women! They are so hardy that, no matter how fast we hurry, we can never get to them before their babies are born!" Pharaoh's plan had involved using the midwives to trick the Hebrew women into thinking their babies were stillborn, and this threw him off his game plan. What did he know about giving birth? He bought their story.

It might even seem a little humorous to us now, but think about what it would have felt like for Shiphrah and Puah. It must have been really frightening to stand before the Pharaoh with a fabricated excuse for not following his orders. They must have realized that he could easily put them to death for this. But they chose to say no to his plan of death and destruction.

And what about Jocheved? She was already a mother, and maybe it was that experience that made her feel determined to carry another baby to term. Or, maybe she didn't have the option to end her pregnancy. It must have taken some significant courage, though, to continue that pregnancy, to take it to full term feeling the eyes of everyone in the community, watching her and wondering: what will she do if it's a boy? And then imagine the courage it must have taken to labor through his birth and receive the crushing news that her littlest one was, in fact, a boy. And he would die.

And how incredibly difficult it must have been to defy the Pharaoh and hide him, doing whatever it would take to keep him safe and without a long-term solution to save his life... Think of her going about her everyday business, caring for her family, doing what needed to be done, while hiding Moses.

And watching her closely as she did this was Moses' sister Miriam. Who knows what she thought as she watched her mother weave the bull rushes together into the basket? She must have at least realized what her mother was going through. And maybe that's what gave her courage that, when her mother told her to place the basket in the Nile, she ran along the riverbank, keeping the bobbing basket in her sight, ready to jump in at even a hint of tipping. Can you imagine when she stumbled upon the Pharaoh's daughter, bathing in a small tidal pool on the riverbank? And then when she saw her little brother floating toward the princess? When Pharaoh's daughter then takes the baby from the water, the little girl has the guts to go to her and suggest her mother, of all people, as a nursemaid for the found baby!

And the fifth woman was the princess of Egypt herself. She must have been aware, of her father's genocidal mandate. And she knew when she saw the baby in the basket that he was a Hebrew child. As a woman of privilege, she was under no obligation to even notice the basket that floated toward her. Or, she could have passed the baby to one of her maids, she still wouldn't have had to participate in her father's policy. But she opened the basket, found a crying child, and she gathered him up in her arms and knowing everything that she knew, still, she saved him. In fact, she used her power and her position to save him! Five amazing women!

Let's consider the relevance of this story today – as we look at the world we still see oppression and fear; death and violence; injustice and inequality. We may not have the power of a Pharaoh or the resources of the rich. But we do have the power to raise our voices to say no, no to oppression and death and injustice and exclusion. And yes to justice and peace... for everyone.

It was Laurel Ulrich who said, "Women who behave rarely make history," but she wasn't the first to express that. It is through quiet, subversive acts by regular people that we change the world. The five women of exodus did this, and countless unnamed others have too. Women and men who behave rarely make history. Or as Margaret Mead famously put it: "Never doubt that a small group of thoughtful, committed citizens can change the world. Indeed, it is the only thing that ever has."

Here is what we can take from the story: the strength to summon just enough courage to live in freedom.

OUR MODERN PLAGUES

We've eaten dinner and shared stories. Because our Seder is about the struggle for freedom and obstacles to overcome, let's remember how fortunate we really are. After enduring slavery, the Israelites fled Egypt and they wandered in the desert, facing hunger and thirst. In our modern world there are many who go hungry every day.

There is a Passover ritual of dipping one's finger into a glass of wine and placing a drop of wine onto a plate… one drop for each of the Ten Plagues. We will use this ritual act, but in our own way, as we will now place a drop of wine to represent obstacles that we must overcome - our modern plagues.

1. Hunger… too many children in America and around the world, go to sleep hungry, which is caused by the next plague …

2. Poverty… the lack of basic human needs at home and abroad including housing, jobs, clean water, and health care.

3. Racism….the belief in the inherent racial inferiority of different groups, leading to systematic oppression, discrimination, violence and death.

Act Now... Save Our earth... Plant a tree

4. Sexism… the belief in the inferiority of girls and women, in large and subtle ways, which leads to unequal pay, denying education and even femicide.

5. Domestic and Sexual Violence… committed against women and girls, men and boys, who are too often silenced or not believed.

6. Homophobia…causing discrimination, hate, even leading to murder and suicide.

7. Genocide… of Indigenous Peoples, the Holocaust, Rwanda and Darfur.

8. Hate Groups and Extremists… skinheads, Aryan Nation, KKK, anti-immigration groups, religious fanatics of all kinds, leading to murder and terrorism.

9. Pollution and Global Warming…the destruction of ou planet, from the polar ice caps to our back yards.

10. Fear… the ultimate plague that divides us and is used by people to manipulate and create mistrust, resulting in backlash and stopping progress.

FOURTH CUP OF WINE:
THE JOURNEY CONTINUES

We drink this cup of wine to loosen our tongues… because we must learn to speak out and speak the truth, about the joy, pain and contradictions that exist in life. We must speak out and challenge the absence of women from traditional texts, history and leadership roles…Continue to organize, march, vote, and support each other and our values…

Fight injustice in its many forms…

Break the silence that masks suffering…

Teach children to pursue justice…

We must create, inspiring others, and ourselves sending our signals into the world…

We must also learn to listen – with compassion and sensitivity…

Recognize that, wherever we are in our lives, we do have the power to effect change…

Honor our past, and envision our future…

And still it may not be enough… but it will be ours.

Printed in the United States
By Bookmasters